AN OPEN BOOK

Unashamed

Audria Murphy-Newton

An Open Book "Unashamed"

Copyright © 2022 All Rights Reserved

Cover Design by Audria Newton

Published in the United States by Audria Newton

All rights reserved. In accordance with the U.S. Copyright Act of 1976, no portion of this book may be reproduced, stored in a retrieval system, or transmitted by any form or by any means electronic, mechanical, photocopying, recording, scanning, or other except for brief bible scriptures quotations in critical reviews or articles without prior written permission from the copyright holder. Thank you for supporting the author's rights.

Contents

Acknowledgments..........................viii

Introduction..................................ix

Poem: I Am Not Ashamed.................xiv

Chapter 1: In Search of Love..............16

Chapter 2: Faced with Rejection and Fear...56

Chapter 3: Depression and Suicide Struggle..76

Chapter 4: Struggle with Sexual Immortality....................................90

Chapter 5: God Spared My Life..........103

Chapter 6: Sufferings and Blessings...114

Chapter 7: More Than Conquer........138

A Prayer for Freedom......................145

Scriptures Recap

Other Books

We should always be opened to helping others overcome their situations by telling our testimonies

Acknowledgments

As I share my life experiences, I cannot do it without honoring my Lord and Savior. God has been so good to me. Without Him, it would not be possible to be a writer/author. I give thanks to Him for using me as a willing vessel to be a living testimony. I understand that my life is not my own, and it is an open book. All glory to the Highest God for blessing me with this gift. I would also like to thank all those who have been a supporter of me, including my readers. Please know that this project was birth from love for you.

Introduction

God intends for us to be a light to the world. He allows us to go through some things to help others. Certain things we deal with seem overwhelming and hard to conquer. Sometimes it feels overwhelming with no way out. But that is when we must seek the Lord. God is the solution to all our troubles. I know because I have been through circumstances that only God could pull me through. And since I have overcome, I must use what I have learned and gone through to help someone else break free from anything that may have them bound.

It is only God who can deliver us out of situations. Sometimes it is easier said than done to trust God, but faith is the key to deliverance. What is faith? According to the Holy Bible scripture, **Hebrews 11:1 says, faith is the substance of things hoped for, the evidence of things not seen.** It is saying that you believe in something that you cannot physically see happening. To you, it may feel impossible, but for God, it is so simple.

I encourage you to put your faith and trust in the Lord if you need anything. It does not matter what it is; God can do it. Some are battling with several situations, whether it is a dream that may seem complicated to accomplish, trying to quit an addiction, wrestling with a spirit, or so on. But I would like to let you know that God can help you get through any circumstance. I faced so many struggles, but I defeated them with the help of God.

I used to be one who was ashamed of some of my battles. I did not want anyone to know. But I realize my life is an open book.

Some things we deal with are not for us but to help others conquer their issues. Being open to testifying about some things we have been through allows others to know there is hope. **Revelation 12:11 says, and they overcame him by the blood of the Lamb, and by the word of their testimony, and they loved not their lives unto death.** After our deliverance, we must be opened books to others. We should confess our faults and continue to witness for Christ to let others know that we are overcomers through Him.

I believe that Christ can use my story to help change lives. Telling my story of struggles and deliverances is my message. I have heard others' testimonies that gave me the confidence to know that God can do the impossible. Also, I have given testimonies where people have told me that my testifying was a need for them. Since then, I have been motivated to express myself and no longer be ashamed of where I may have fallen short. If telling my story helps others to become free, then it is my duty to spread the word. I pray that this book of testimonies will help heal others.

I Am Not Ashamed

Matthew 5:14-16 declares that I am the light of the world, a city set on a hill cannot be hidden; nor does anyone light a basket, but on the lampstand, and it gives light to all who are in the house. Let your light shine before men in such a way that they may see your good works and glorify your Father who is in heaven.

Therefore, I must shed my light to the world by speaking on my testimonies, being unashamed, letting the world know, that they too can be free, free from what holds them captive, free from negativity that has been passed down from generations, free from the lies of the enemy, saying you can't be free,

free from worrying about the thoughts and opinions of others, and free from being ashamed of the past. I am not ashamed because I am now living in liberty, and you too shall be free

AN OPEN BOOK

UNASHAMED

Chapter 1
In Search of Love

Unashamed

Love is patient, love is kind. It does not envy, it does not boast, it is not proud. It does not dishonor others, it is not self-seeking, it is not easily angered, it keeps no record of wrongs. Love does not delight in evil but rejoices with the truth. It always protects, always trusts, always hopes, always perseveres. 1 Corinthians 13:4-7

A four-letter word called love is so sensitive but powerful. It can be so kind, beautiful, and sweet. But also, it may bring about pain and hurt. So, how could this small

AN OPEN BOOK

In Search of Love

but muscled word cause pain and hurt? Depending on the situation, relationships in families, marriages, friendships, and etcetera can produce many different emotions. I know because I rode on the love rollercoaster. It left me with mixed feelings and emotions.

I grew up in a family of ten children, and life was hard. The biggest obstacle was constantly moving from place to place. I am uncertain why we moved so many times throughout the years, but it was very frustrating. Another issue was my father was not always there for us. If you read Unforgiveness, Guilt, and Regrets, I shared in that book how my feelings towards my dad,

AN OPEN BOOK

In Search of Love

did not precisely describe the word love. The love I had for him was buried under some anger. Growing up I felt as though my father did not love us. Watching other kids that had a close relationship with their fathers pushed me to be a little jealous. It was not hateful jealousy, but a form of wishing my father would show my siblings and me more affection. Even though he would spend time with us sometimes, there was still a void I had. I wanted to have a close relationship with him. The thing about him was that he did not express the word love much. It had me feeling neglected on the inside.

God is our first love, but earthly, I

AN OPEN BOOK

In Search of Love

believe that a father should be a girl's, first love. A daughter should be treated with love from her dad so that when she begins to date, she will know how a man should treat her. See, in my case, that did not happen. The love I was looking for from my dad, I began to search for it in others. I grew up unsure of how a man should express love. Without a demonstration of love, it left me lost and confused. Once I began dating, I accepted much less than what I deserved.

After years of dating, I hopped from relationship to relationship. When a guy treated me wrong, I stayed because I did not want to be alone. I made it easy for a man to

AN OPEN BOOK

In Search of Love

manipulate me. I had relationships where the guys would treat me respectfully. Then suddenly, they would change into someone I did not recognize. Things such as cheating, verbal abuse, lies, and manipulation would reveal themselves. With all that happening to me, bitterness developed in my heart. I would push away a good man who came into my life because I could not discern what was real or a lie.

I fell in love easily and quickly, which left me in a powerless position. A man can tell when a woman is vulnerable, and some use it to get what they want out of her. A lot of people say that love is blind. However, I do not believe that. My belief is that, just

In Search of Love

because a person may love someone does not mean they are blind to things that are revealed. It is a choice to put up with certain things and folks that are no good for us. Sometimes people can use love as a substitution for loneliness or fear. I believe that love can have someone addicted for several reasons. An example of this could be, searching for love. It is a hunger to some people. For me, I wanted to be loved so badly, that I would fall in love and see that the person was up to no good. So, since I was hungry to be loved, I chose to stay in a toxic relationship. Therefore, I was not blinded by love, I was afraid of being lonely. I was caught up in just having someone, therefore I

In Search of Love

accepted a lie of false love. Love will make you have standards and know who you are. To others, they can feel as though being treated wrongly is deserving of them. It is not necessarily that they are blind, it may be due to them being raised a certain way or it's something they encountered for so long. It keeps them in a powerless position of accepting that type of abuse. They may not see that they deserve better or can do better. In my situation, I was not blind, I was craving a love I always wanted and needed from my father. I realized that my whole life, I was chasing after a lie of love that did not exist.

My life has been a rollercoaster of

AN OPEN BOOK

In Search of Love

being in love too many times. I tried living my life in Christ and doing the right thing, but still wanting love caused me to do some things outside God's will. I was having sex outside of the marriage covenant. This act pressured me into a marriage I was not ready for. My husband and I were immature and did things to hurt one another. The main reason I married him was that I was struggling with having sex unmarried. I loved him, but the marriage was not the right move at the time. Lots of opinions say that sex should not be the only reason for marriage, and that is true, but it was not the only reason for me. Again, I loved my husband, but that was not enough. One day before I agreed to

In Search of Love

marry him, I had decided to end our relationship. I no longer wanted to live in sin. We had a discussion one day about me not wanting to engage in sex. He was not in agreement with that, so I told him I wanted to break up. I began walking towards the door to leave when he came after me and told me he did not want to lose me. He then dropped on one knee and proposed. I said yes out of desperation and knowing that we were not ready for that next chapter of our lives. All I wanted was to live righteously, yet one of my battles was having sexual relations. So, I thought that marriage was the right thing to do. Besides, there is a scripture in the bible that says in **1 Corinthians 7:8-9: I say**

AN OPEN BOOK

In Search of Love

therefore to the unmarried and widows, it is good for them to abide even as I. But if they cannot contain, let them marry; for it is better to marry than to burn. I took that scripture seriously. The whole chapter 7 speaks on marriages and the unmarried. The unmarried should remain single and not engage in sexual activities. Many people may look at this scripture differently, but for me, it was imperative.

How I Met My Ex-husband

My ex-husband and myself knew each other since childhood. My parents moved us to the same town where he and his family lived. It was in 1996, and on my first

In Search of Love

day of school, I got put into his class. I saw him and had the smallest crush on him as a little girl. Time went by and in high school, I moved away to another town. Then two years later, he and his family relocated to where I lived. I had a boyfriend, but we had broken up. Two weeks after the breakup, we exchanged numbers and dated up until a few months after graduating. We kept in touch for a while and still had intercourse. His sister told us one time that if we did not stop, I would get pregnant, which managed to be true. I was with someone else at the time I was pregnant. I thought it was my boyfriend's baby, but it turned out to be my ex-boyfriend's baby. The guy who I was with

AN OPEN BOOK

In Search of Love

was cheating on me during our whole relationship. I found out, and so I decided to cheat on him. I chose to cheat with my ex because I still loved him. Long story short, I finally ended our relationship. And after finding out my son was my ex's, we decided to work things out. Once my son's father and I got back together, that was around the time I was trying to live a righteous life. So, as I said, we got married, even though it was not the right decision. Two years later, we had a daughter. Then unexpectedly, our marriage began to fall apart. With both of us being immature, we argued frequently and

In Search of Love

continuously remained mad at each other. Then, infidelity took place from both parties which led to a divorce.

Over the years, we both moved on with our lives and got involved with other people. My journey continued the search for love. I still had a void in my heart. After dating a guy for two years, our relationship ended. Later, I got involved with a man who worked for the same company as me, but he got fired some months later. We went out for a few months, but I did not want to be with him. We never told each other we were in a relationship. We were just chatting and went out on a date a few times as friends. I met a

In Search of Love

few of his family members but never clarified we were dating. He started claiming me as his girlfriend so, I decided to give it a try. Things were fine for a while, but we decided that being friends would be better for us, so we broke up and stayed friends. Little did I know, the man I met would turn into someone different. There was a secret about him that came to the light.

The True Identity Revealed

We must be aware of wolves in sheep clothing. People pretend like they are harmless but are in disguised, they are evil.

One day he called me out of the blue and said he wanted to go out for his birthday, so I agreed. He was overly drunk when I picked him up. We went to the bowling alley,

In Search of Love

and that was an embarrassing experience because he was so loud and kept falling on the floor. So, after that, we went to get a bite to eat. I glanced at a man who walked by with a woman in the restaurant. Suddenly my ex became so jealous, demanded to know what I was looking at, got up, and knocked my cup off the table. He then grabbed my keys from the table and walked out of the door. I was humiliated and apologized to the couple sitting next to us because the cup hit one of them. So, I ran after him, ashamed of the scene that he caused. I tried relentlessly to get my keys back from him. I did not want him to drive because he was intoxicated. He

AN OPEN BOOK

In Search of Love

became extremely aggressive, and he would not give my keys to me. I got in the car on the passenger side, and he drove off. Thankfully, he drove safely to his house. He got out of the car, and I said to him that I never want to see him again. As I was about to leave, he quickly grabbed my cell phone and would not return it to me. The phone was a brand-new phone and a gift from someone. So, I tried to convince him to return it to me, but I was unsuccessful. He took my phone across the street to a vacant yard. It was dark, and I could not see what he had done with my phone. He came back into his yard and sat down in a chair by the door. He began to taunt me by saying I would never see my phone

In Search of Love

again, and some other mean things I could not remember. As I looked at him, all I could see was an evil demonic look on his face. It was as though his whole countenance had changed from him to a different person. It had come to my mind that he lived with his aunt. I went inside the house to see if I could get her to help me get my phone. She tried to persuade him to give the phone back but could not. She called his mother, who came over and she could not get the phone either. His mother sorrowfully looked at me and said, "go home, and I will get your phone when he is sober." I left upset and disappointed. I refused to allow him to keep what belonged to me, so I returned to the

In Search of Love

house. His mom was gone, and his aunt was in the house. He was still outside, so I parked on the side of the road. I got out of the car and asked him would he please return my phone. Without saying a word, he hopped in my car on the passenger side and told me to drive, but I would not do it. I walked to the side of the car and tried to make him get out. He would not budge. After a few minutes, he got out. I stood by the trunk of the car and sobbed. At that point, I was exhausted and tired. It was late, like one or two a.m. I asked him one last time to give me my phone because I needed it. He said no. So, I fell to the ground as an act, hoping that would convince him to feel sorry for me and

In Search of Love

be remorseful. He did begin to panic but instead, he picked me up and put me in the car. Then he got in and began to drive. He drove up to a gas station, then said, "do not try anything; you can call the police, but I will deny it." Some individuals probably would ask why I did not leave when I had a chance, and I could have gotten another phone. Well, I was ashamed and did not want anyone to know what had happened. I knew I would have to tell someone if I would have gone home without my phone. But the main reason was due to guilt and shame and because I did not leave, I went through torment and a nightmare.

In Search of Love

The First Attack

After he got back into the car, he pulled up to a hotel. He forced me to go into a room with him and raped me. He did not beat me or anything, but he made me have intercourse with him. I pleaded with him to please stop but he did not, and he was too strong for me to push him off me. I cried all night. Once he was done, I could have gotten away and gotten my keys while he was asleep, but I was drained, weak, and scared. I was so tired that I felt lifeless and could not move. The following day, he was sober and tried to apologize. I did not say a word to him, and he had a worried look on his face. In my

In Search of Love

mind, I wanted revenge and to do something about it, but I could not. I was afraid of what else he might do. I took him home, and his mom was there. I did not mention to her what he had done to me, but I did explain why I had come back. She then got my phone from him and handed it to me. She said, "I am so sorry this happened to you; this was not the first time he did this." She began to tell me about another woman he had attacked before while he was under the influence. She also said, that is my son, and I love him, but I advise you to leave and never look back. I took her advice and cut him entirely off, but that was not the end of this nightmare.

AN OPEN BOOK

In Search of Love

He persistently called my phone, drastically trying to apologize. I said to him, "never contact me again." He responded angrily, saying, "I can not keep his kids away from him." I was shocked at his statement because for one my kids were not his and he had only been around them once. The last thing I told him was he would never see them again, and I hung up the phone. Unfortunately, he continued to call me, but I would not answer. Two weeks went by, and a weird feeling came over me while I was at work. During my lunch break, I was talking to a co-worker, and I told her I had an odd feeling. I felt uneasy as if something was about to happen and I was correct.

AN OPEN BOOK

In Search of Love

After work, I got into my car and pulled out of my parking space. Suddenly, he rushed his car behind me as I was backing out of my parking space. I could not believe it when I noticed that it was him. I did not think I would see him again. Finally, he backed up to let me out. He got out of his car and signaled me to pull my car over. There were quite a few people outside, so I decided to pull over. Once I parked my car, he got in on the passenger side. He handed me some flowers, balloons, and a dinner he had bought for me. He said, "I did not want you to have to cook when you get home, so I bought you and the kids something to eat." I was thinking to myself, this man is crazy. I began

In Search of Love

to look around in the parking lot to find help from anyone close by. He finally got out of the car and came to my side. I had the window rolled down. One of my supervisors was walking by. He noticed my ex, so he suspiciously asked me was I ok. I told him yes. He then asked me am I sure. I said yes because there were people outside. He said ok; let him know if I needed anything, then walked into the building. I began looking back at two ladies across the parking lot, they were standing at their car. He then began to act jealous, and he yelled at me saying, "who are you looking at; I knew you had another man out here." He said that referring to a male friend who was a good friend of mines.

AN OPEN BOOK

In Search of Love

It was at that moment, I figured out he was drunk again. I should have paid close attention to how he was when he worked with me. He would feel some type of way when he saw me talking to other men on the job.

Signs of Jealousy

While working together, he was so jealous. He would spy on me and say something to me about how he saw me talking to other guys. He would always accuse me of cheating with someone else. His focus was on one main man who was only a friend. We became friends because he had a business selling cable, and I became a customer. My boyfriend would diligently

In Search of Love

accuse us of mixing business with pleasure. His jealousy was so out of control, and I knew this when he accused me of giving him an STD. I went to get tested to prove to him; I was not cheating. The results came back negative. I confronted him, and he had nothing to say even though he was the one who cheated. Most of the time as people say, when someone constantly accuses, they are the ones who be cheating. This statement described him. Yet, he persistently would be angry when other men on the job approached me, even when it was innocent. I should have recognized the signs, but I paid it no mind.

The Second Attack

In Search of Love

Now back to the incident, after he yelled at me, he reached his hand through the window and grabbed a hand full of my hair with one hand and my car keys with the other. Once he let go of my hair, I jumped out of the car and ran. He then proceeded to chase me, and I ran inside of the building. My supervisor was standing in the hallway. He asked me what was wrong. I explained to him the horrific situation, and he immediately called the police. We went outside to wait for the police to come. My ex drove off in my car up the road, came back, and left my car parked in the middle of the parking lot. He got into his car and drove away. I ran to my car and noticed he had taken my keys. When

In Search of Love

the police arrived, they took down my information and filed a report. Once the officers left, my friend came outside to check on me, and he offered to get me another key made for my vehicle. We called around to get quotes, and it was expensive. Because it was expensive, thankfully, God moved on my supervisor's heart to help with the cost. Finally, I had enough money to get another key, but the locksmith could not make the key until the following morning. My friend offered me a ride home, but I had to wait on him to get off work which was about three hours away. He had gotten off work at eight p.m. and we went to get something to eat. Later, I had him drop me off at my sister's

AN OPEN BOOK

In Search of Love

apartment in the same city where I worked because I lived about 45 minutes away.

The next morning, my friend came to pick me up. He drove me back to my car to meet the locksmith. Once I got my key, I left and went straight home. I never told a soul about the incident except for one person, and it was my sister who's house I went to. The following week, I went to get my police report and to formally press charges. His family called me and apologized to me for what he did to me. They also begged me not to press charges. His mom asked me to give him a chance to go away to rehab to get help. I agreed to allow him to go get help, but I

In Search of Love

said, "he will have to pay me the money back for the car key." We went to court a few days later. The judge asked me did I want to press charges, and I said no, only because his family pleaded with me not to. I told him I would give him a chance at rehab, but I needed him to return the expense for my car key. His family gathered up the money to pay me. And I never heard from him again until months later. Almost a year went by, and my ex reached out to me through Facebook messenger. He told me he turned his life around and gave his life to Christ. The rehab helped him change his ways. He then said how sorry he was and asked if we could go

In Search of Love

out again. I nicely declined, told him I forgive him, and congratulated him on giving his life to God and left it at that. After that, I never heard from him again.

I know most people probably would have pressed charges, but I do believe in second chances. He was a good person who allowed the demons of alcohol to control him. Forgiveness is always essential, but it does not mean you have to keep a connection with folks. I would say that if he was sober while attacking me, then I would have sent him to jail. Demons are real, and they do not care how they affect people. Sometimes people allow demons to have dominion over

In Search of Love

them. In other words, they take possession of individuals' minds, and when they are possessed, it is not them; it is the demon making them do things. And that is what happened to him. The demons of the alcohol had him possessed, and for that reason, I decided to give him a chance to change. That was only the love and grace of God I let him have a second chance. There's no excuse for what he did, yet I had compassion on him because I know I am far from being perfect.

I often think of how many times I have wronged people. It may not have been hurting someone physically, but verbally, I have. Also, I search for myself and

AN OPEN BOOK

In Search of Love

understand how many times I have hurt God. Sadly, we judge others and say what they have done wrong to us, but what have we done to others? How many times have we disobeyed God? Or how many times have we turned our backs on God? But He still forgave us. People forget that God has feelings too, and therefore, this is one reason I do not judge anyone. I have had my share of hurting others knowingly and unknowingly. Also, it is only God who can judge others, not man.

Everyone has had some type of addiction in their lifetime, whether long-term or short-term. Sin itself is an addiction and love especially are one. And one of my

AN OPEN BOOK

In Search of Love

obsessions were receiving love from the wrong people. Before anyone gets to know Christ, repentance is required because of the sinful nature within us. Our flesh desires to sin, but it is our spirit that yearns to live righteously. There is only one perfect man who never sinned, and that man was Jesus.

The Next Relationship

I went on proceeding to seek love. My friend from the job took me out on dates a few times. He treated me like a queen even though we were just friends. He was everything I ever wanted in a man. I found myself falling in love with him because no man had ever treated me the way he did. He

In Search of Love

genuinely cared about me with no strings attached. You can feel and tell whether someone's love is genuine or have a motive. Some months into us growing close, we decided to date. The only problem was, he was not living for God. We dated for about a year, but God spoke to me and told me to let him go because he was not the man for me. It took me a while to mention to him that I had to end our relationship. As much as I did not want to let him go, I had to listen to the voice of God.

After a couple more failed relationships, I told God I am going to wait on Him. I began to seek God more and be

In Search of Love

patient. I was fed up with having different men in and out of my life. That was not the example I wanted my daughter or my son to see. I purposed in my mind that I will not date another man until He approved it.

The Man Sent from God

One day, a friend of my sister's sent me a friend request on Facebook. I declined because I did not know him. My sister called me and told me who he was, so I accepted it. He began to minister to me and speak blessings over my life. I knew he had to be from God because the things he said were things I never shared with anyone, and he did not know me at all. We chatted for some

In Search of Love

months and began praying and reading the word of God together. I never had anyone take time to read the word of God with me or pray for me. It was something I always longed for in a man.

Out of nowhere, I felt myself having strong feelings for him. It was a different kind of feeling like it was pure and uncontrollable. I cried like a baby and prayed so hard to God. I did not want to make any more mistakes with dating the wrong man. I told God, if this man is not the man for me, please cut him out of my life. Instead, the love progressed. All that I have been through with men had me skeptical about him at first. But we became

In Search of Love

friends before we became lovers. We decided to get married some months later. The day I got married, it was just me, my husband, and the pastor. It felt so good to be married and have someone who loves me. I knew it was God because out of nowhere, I began to cry and felt the Holy Spirit come upon me. It was a peaceful feeling as if a burden had lifted off me. Then I heard the voice of God say to me; now I can get the glory out of your life. I understood why He said that. I no longer have to battle with having sex out of marriage and bounce to another relationship. All the times of dating the wrong men, God could not completely do what needed to be done on the inside of me until I was in right standing with

In Search of Love

Him. If I felt uneasy about marrying him, I would not have. God approved it, and that is all that mattered to me.

The love I longed for I never got until God made me realize who I was and whose I was. Yes, I am happily married, but even my husband's love does not complete me. Although I craved that love from my dad, God showed me that He is the one true love. Now that I am wiser and living for Christ, I understand that love can never be chased or given until you know who God is. His love is real, right, pure, and unconditional. No one's love can never compare to God's love. Even while accepting God's love, you must love

In Search of Love

yourself. You may often hear the saying, "self-love is the best love." While that is a true statement, loving yourself will keep you from facing so many heartaches in relationships. When you love yourself, you will not accept anything or allow people to treat you any kind of way. So, if you are seeking love, I dare you to seek God's love first and everything else will follow.

Chapter 2
Faced with Rejection and Fear

Unashamed

Rejection is something that I have faced most of my life. It is an emotion of feeling unwanted or unaccepted. Growing up, I did not realize a part of my love searching journey came from rejection. The love my dad did not express was not the only reason for being challenged with rejection but being rejected by other people played a role. For so long, I tried to fit in with other people, even as an adult. It seemed as if I never could find a real true friend.

I got bullied and made fun of when I

Faced with Rejection and Fear

was a young girl. When I was in the first grade, I can remember this bigger girl who I thought was my friend. She would always get me into trouble because I was afraid of her, and I just wanted a friend. She was the only one I talked to a lot, so I did everything she told me to do. How she got me into trouble was she told me to steal something out of the classroom for her, and there was a time she dared me to jump out of the girl's restroom window and I did. The principal came walking up the breezeway and caught me trying to jump back into the window. Being small as I was and young, I did not know any better.

Faced with Rejection and Fear

The bullying lasted for a while until an older sister of mines found out and demanded that she stop or else. After that, I never had a problem with her. But she was not the only one who bullied me; other kids would laugh at me as well. The kids would pick at how I wore my hair, some of the type of clothing I wore, and the way I walked. I have scoliosis, which is a condition causing my back to be crooked. I could have gotten surgery but, I never had any problems with pain. Also, I never wanted to wear a back braise which would have given my back support to grow straight as I aged. I knew that I would be that loser kid as being a target to

AN OPEN BOOK

Faced with Rejection and Fear

really be picked on. I was already being teased enough every day.

As I grew older, I was still the girl who had gotten picked at from middle school to high school. In my eighth-grade year, my family moved to another town. Lo, and behold, I was a target of being criticized. There was one girl I thought became my friend. She would treat me nicely and help me with some of my schoolwork. One day this boy in the class who was a class clown was making fun of me. He then said to the girl, that is your friend. She then said, "no, she is not." I could not believe what she had said. It hurt me to my soul. After that day, I did not

AN OPEN BOOK

Faced with Rejection and Fear

say much to her again. I could not believe how she turned on me. I talked to other students but none of them was in my class. I just kept to myself.

Another incident was, there was this boy who wanted to date me at the same school. He had just broken up with a girl. I accepted his invitation to be his girlfriend. We talked for some weeks, and suddenly, his ex-girlfriend and some other students interfered with our relationship. Some said, "he did not like me, he only felt sorry for me, and he was cheating. I confronted him about it in a letter because we exchanged letters every day since we were not in the same

AN OPEN BOOK

__Faced with Rejection and Fear__

class. He wrote me back and broke up with me because he said he did not feel we should be together because I did not trust him. After our relationship ended, other students began laughing at me. His ex-girlfriend walked by the classroom and said, "Hey you girl, he (I cannot include the guy's name) said you stink." A few days later, I saw him hugged up with his ex. I felt so devastated and rejected. My life felt like a girl you would see in a movie being bullied. Some of them pretended to like me only to make me look bad. My little heart was crushed. There were some days I just wanted to hide.

Some other things that have happened

Faced with Rejection and Fear

to make me feel unwanted were not being chosen as partners for an activity. I never had anyone I felt I could call a true friend throughout my life at school and in adulthood. I have always been shy and a person of few words. I think that my being not so talkative caused me not to be a favorite person. I have even lost relationships with good men because I was not good at holding a conversation. But, at different times and places, I would feel counted out because I would be the last one standing without a partner. There were even times I was surrounded by people sitting at tables together, and I sat alone. I would think to myself, why am I never chosen. Or why no

AN OPEN BOOK

Faced with Rejection and Fear

one wants to sit with me. I may have been dramatic or too sensitive, but I felt that way because I never had any friends I could often talk to. Now, I have had few people I can call a true friend, but it would be a friendship where we would go weeks or months without talking. There has always been a little girl on the inside of me who wanted to have a best friend who I can confide in and who will be like a sister to me. When times came around as though I did, the friendship will go the other way.

In high school, I met a girl who became my best friend. I would go to her house and sleep over. I began calling her

Faced with Rejection and Fear

mom, my second mom. We stayed friends for years even after graduation. She was one I believed would be my best friend forever. I loved her like a sister. Meanwhile, as we grew older, we began to drift apart. For years, I would go to her house and check on her. Twice we lived right up the road from each other, and I never got the same treatment. Our friendship was one-sided. Every now and then she would call but for some reason, she changed. She was no longer that best friend I met in high school. When I would want us to hang out, there would be an excuse or a no-show. After a while, I just stopped trying to convince her to do things with me. Some years later, we completely lost touch. A year

AN OPEN BOOK

Faced with Rejection and Fear

went by, and she was on my mind. That same day, I ran into her at a store. Me being who I am trying to mend our friendship, I started back calling her and checking on her. That lasted only a few weeks. I was going through some things in my life and my schedule was always full. One day after two to three weeks, I reached out to her to see how she was doing. She did not sound too excited to hear from me. For one, she had erased my number and weeks back had my number blocked but blamed her daughter. I wanted to believe that was the case but, in my mind, I knew better. When I called her, I asked if I could come by to see her and her kids because I was right down the road from her house at a laundry

Faced with Rejection and Fear

mat. She said she was about to leave and take her kids to the park. I said, well maybe I and my kids could join them. She hesitated as if she did not want us to come, so I took it as a sign, it's time for me to depart ways from her again for good. Later I received a text that there was a change of plans and I just responded ok. After that, I never spoke to her again.

I prayed and asked God some time ago, why it is always hard for me to make friends or keep a close friend. He said, you are different; I have chosen you to be set apart. People sometimes are only part of your life for a season, especially when you

Face with Rejection and Fear

are a child of God and is chosen. Also, there are people we outgrow. In other words, people come and go in our lives. God must protect the anointing that His people carry. Everyone will not understand it or be able to handle what God do in our lives. I cannot say that it did not bother me to lose a friendship I had for years, but I understand the assignment on my life. Before I got to the point of understanding the mandate on my life, I always felt lonely like an outcast. I believe with love searching, from a child on up, I never wanted to be alone.

Loneliness can come from rejection. Rejection had me bound for so long, and it

Faced with Rejection and Fear

made me feel like no one loved me or wanted me. Also, it had me feeling like I needed validation from others. I went through a phase of life feeling unpretty, and I would compare myself to other women. I had a lack of confidence and low self-esteem. I would not speak up for myself, and when I may have wanted to do or accomplish things, I would allow intimidation to step in the way to stop me. I allowed others to dictate who I am and what I should do with my life. The fear of what others thought about me was a major stumbling block for me. Believe it or not, so much in my life has been affected by feeling rejected. For years, I felt trapped by rejection which had the best of me. It took God to

Faced with Rejection and Fear

deliver me from it. Because of wanting love and friends, I have made unwise choices in my life due to being bound by these spirits. But I am grateful to God that I am no longer bound by rejection or loneliness.

If you are dealing with rejection, I want to let you know that you are not alone. God is always with you. If you feel like you cannot trust anyone else or maybe feel like no one loves you, God is love, and you can always trust Him. I had to learn that God will never leave me or forsake me no matter who comes or goes in my life. Scripture **Deuteronomy 31:6 says, Be strong and courageous. Do not be afraid or terrified**

Faced with Rejection and Fear

because of them, for the Lord your God goes with you; He will never leave you nor forsake you. Please believe that you do not have to allow being rejected or alone to get you down or cause you to give up. Everyone is not going to agree with you, like you, or even some may leave, but in the end, it is God who will always be there. Long as you have Him, nothing else matters.

Fear

Along with rejection and loneliness, I dealt with fear. Fear is one of the strongest strongholds that have people procrastinating. It keeps people from pursuing their visions and dreams. Also, when it comes to ministry,

Faced with Rejection and Fear

people do not walk in their true calling because of fear. I am a witness to that. I know some things that God has called me to do spiritually and naturally but being afraid of the opinions of others and not being good enough held me back. But, according to scripture **2 Timothy 1:7, it says, For God hath not given us the spirit of fear; but of power, and of love, and of a sound mind.** God has given us the power to overcome any fear but instead of trusting Him and believing it, we continue to walk in defeat. I am reminded of Moses in the Bible, that when God called him to lead the children of Israel out of bondage, he was afraid **(Exodus Chapter 3-4)**. What made him fearful was,

Faced with Rejection and Fear

he was worried about what he would say, how the people would perceive him, and what he was to do. Then God had to remind him who He was and that He would be there with him to guide him. A lot of us are like Moses or have been in that place as Moses, questioning God instead of trusting Him.

Fear has so many individuals afraid of being rejected, unwanted, being alone, not being good enough, or etcetera. As I mentioned above, for years from being a child, I walked in rejection, and because of that, I never wanted to be alone. I always wanted to be accepted and have someone to love me. I yearned and searched for attention, love, and validation from man, instead of

AN OPEN BOOK

Faced with Rejection and Fear

receiving real love from God. So much time in my life passed me by because the opinions of others had me scared to express myself and do the things that I know I was called to do. I allowed so much manipulation to control me and some people knew that. When people can read that someone is fearful, some will take advantage of that and use it to their advantage. Therefore, overcoming fear is so important. The only way to conquer fear is to face it and trust that God is with you.

Before I published my first book, some doubt and fear were holding me back from publishing it. I was worried about whether people would read it, not getting any

AN OPEN BOOK

Faced with Rejection and Fear

sales, or it was not a good read. I repeatedly received confirmation to proceed with publishing my book. I had to conquer my fear and step out on faith. Once I published my book, I received nothing but good feedback. It was my intention to only have women readers, but I had a review from a male who read my book and enjoyed it. So many people go through unforgiveness which was the topic of my book, and it has helped uplift many. I had to understand that my book is a ministry and then a business. Although making money from it is a blessing but my focus is to change lives. I put my story out so that others who may be going through the

Faced with Rejection and Fear

same thing can know that there is hope and a way out.

Again, if you are battling with fear right now, the best way to have authority over it is to face it. It does not matter what others think or even what you may think. If God told you to do something or you feel led to do something, go for it. Don't question it or procrastinate or you will walk in defeat for the rest of your life until you face it. Go after that business, book, promotion on your job, or whatever it is you are trying to accomplish. At the end of the day, nothing or no one is standing in your way except you.

Chapter 3
Depression and Suicide Struggle

Unashamed

Depression is an emotional disorder that causes a feeling of sadness. There are many causes of depression. It can come from relationships, circumstances, anxiety, and etcetera. I know the feeling of being in that state, and it is not a good feeling. I remember several times; I fell into a sense of being depressed. And for many, depression is not easy to escape. It took me a while to overcome it. I cannot remember the first time I experienced feeling depressed; but I do

AN OPEN BOOK

Depression and Suicide Struggle

remember a few times I was in a confrontation with depression. If you understand spirituality, we all know that depression is a spirit that comes from the devil. Depression is easy to hide as well. People can look at you and think that you are happy, but inside, there is a feeling of emptiness. I have been there, where I was smiling on the outside, but on the inside, I was so miserable.

The Year of 2006, two years after high school, I lived in Norcross (Atlanta) Ga, with an older sister. I met a guy who started off treating me nice but then months later he changed. I went to a doctor's appointment

Depression and Suicide Struggle

one day to get a pap smear. A few days later, I got a phone call from the doctor, and she told me that I had contracted an STD. It was curable, but still, I was devastated. I could not believe that he had cheated on me and given me a disease but guess what, I stayed with him.

Being young and naïve persuaded me to stay in a relationship with him. One day, I found out I was pregnant. I told my boyfriend about the pregnancy, and I thought that would maybe change him from being so cruel to being loving. He did not care, he still disrespected me. Over the months, stress got the best of me, leading me to have a

Depression and Suicide Struggle

miscarriage. I was so crushed. I even became angry with God. That was the most depressing time of my life. I was so depressed that I did not even recognize the person I had become. I questioned God as to why He took my baby away from me. He showed me that I put my boyfriend before my child, which made me not want my child. Had I gotten out of my relationship and thought about taking care of my baby, she would be here. It would have been a girl. My boyfriend and I broke up weeks after the miscarriage. God then had to take me through a healing process. That was one of the darkest times in my life. I had lost focus on who I was. When God healed me, I had more clarity on how severe my

AN OPEN BOOK

Depression and Suicide Struggle

depression was. I was so glad God set me free from that bondage, but I had a visit from depression again years later.

I was sitting on the couch at home one day. My son was at school, and my daughter was just a baby. I was going through a separation during my first marriage. I felt all alone and down in my spirit. Not only that, but I was also wrestling with trying to live my life right with the Lord. My walk with God was a real struggle for a long time. I wanted to do right, but it seemed like I could never get to that point where I needed to be. Suddenly, thoughts of suicide began to cross my mind. I heard a voice, which was the devil

Depression and Suicide Struggle

saying to me, run into the highway and end your life. I lived close to a remarkably busy highway, where the traffic was heavy. And as I sat there, I was thinking of throwing myself out there to be hit by a vehicle. I became afraid of my thoughts so; I began to cry out to God for help. I was ok after that, but it was not the end of my depression. That was not the only time I faced depression on and off for the same reason over the years, "my walk with God." I wanted so badly to please God. I would do good for a while, then the next I was backsliding. Bad as I wanted to live right, it was a real wrestle for me. There are regulations and restrictions when living for Christ. Some of those commands are letting

Depression and Suicide Struggle

go of things and people that you are used to. On the journey of being a Christian, it is not easy because denying yourself is a requirement. The flesh and the spirit war against one another **(Galatians 5:17)**. They cannot mix or get along with one another.

The flesh is against God, but the spirit is for God. The flesh wants us to hold on to stuff and individuals God tells us to get rid of.

Many times, I wrestled with doing right and still doing the things of the world. I had it so bad that I would cry, asking God to end my life. I did not have the confidence to live for God. I kept falling short of His glory

__Depression and Suicide Struggle__

and displeasing Him. Even though I know God is forgiving, I had a hard time accepting His forgiveness. I knew I would keep messing up. There were days when I would fall into sin, and after I sinned, suicide would cross my mind. I said to myself; there is no point in living since I keep sinning. I have never been the one who wants to be a hypocrite. It is dangerous having one foot in the church and the other in the world. I knew that if God were to return at that moment, I would not make it into heaven.

Some people go to church and act one way, but at home, they live another way. God will not have us be lukewarm.

AN OPEN BOOK

Depression and Suicide Struggle

Either we will be cold or hot.

Ending my life just seemed like the easiest way out. I did not want to keep sinning and displeasing God. Then God reminded me of **2 Corinthians 12:9: And He said unto me, My grace is sufficient for thee, for my strength is made perfect in weakness. Most gladly, therefore will I rather glory in my infirmities, that the power of Christ may rest upon me.** This scripture shows me that I cannot do things in my own strength. Relying on the strength and mercy of God is the only way I could defeat my sins. And even when you keep falling, you cannot stay down in pity. You must get up and keep moving

AN OPEN BOOK

Depression and Suicide Struggle

forward.

Going through a divorce was another contribution to depression. Once my divorce was completed, I moved in with my younger sister. I was going through financial hardship for years. I felt like God was continually blessing all my siblings and I was being looked over. It felt like they could easily find jobs that paid well, but I had difficulty finding a job or jobs with decent pay. I asked God, why do I have it so hard. He told me that because I have made you the backbone of your family. Meaning I was always praying so hard for my family and tried to keep us glued together. The rest of my siblings

Depression and Suicide Struggle

pray for our family a lot as well, but it was something that God was trying to do through me. For some reason I always felt counted out from the rest of my siblings. I often thought to myself, it's not fair how they all can be so blessed and easily get things that they want. God was wanting to do some things in my life to build me up spiritually, but I was being prideful and disobedient. I did not fully understand who I was in God at the time until years later.

Sometimes we go through afflictions, and it seems like others around us are being blessed. But we still need to trust God and know He has a plan for our lives. In due

Depression and Suicide Struggle

time, He will give you the desires of your heart when you are faithful to Him.

What helped me to overcome this depression was, I was sitting on the couch holding my daughter. She was two or three years old at the time. She grabbed my chin, lifted it, and began to talk to me. I did not understand what she was saying, but I know she knew I was depressed. I cried because she gave me hope. That night I went to church and a prophetess said, your daughter worries about you. Sometimes God would use our children to encourage us. For me, there have been multiple times I wanted to give up but thinking about my kids would motivate me to

Depression and Suicide Struggle

keep pushing. Scripture **Psalm 8:2 says Out of the mouth of babes and sucklings hast thou ordained strength because of thine enemies, that thou mightiest still the enemy and the avenger.** This scripture means that even though children may be young, they can be incredibly wise. In my time of trouble, God used my daughter to encourage me. Some children have a soul of an elderly person, and my daughter is one of them. Another time He used her was when she gave some encouraging words to the church congregation at bible study one night. She stated that **we must walk by faith and not by sight (2 Corinthians 5:7).** It was an encouragement to us all. As adults, we cannot

Depression and Suicide Struggle

be so prideful to where we cannot receive words spoken from a child because God uses who He pleases to get His gospel out. I am so thankful that God used my daughter to help me overcome depression.

The devil wants people to stay down and depressed. His job is to deceive and make you feel as though there is no way out or you cannot be delivered. **But Greater is He that is in you than he that is in the world, 1 John 4:4.** God has given us the power and strength to overrule any sin. And depression cannot oppress you if you give it over to God. I had to learn to let go and let God strengthen me.

Chapter 4
Struggle with Sexual Immortality

Unashamed

Sex can be a beautiful thing, only when it is right. Intercourse is meant just for those who are married. Yet, many are committing adultery every day by having sexual relations without being husband and wife. Sometimes sex can have a stronghold on people for several reasons. And knowingly or not, some people battle with a sex demon. I know because I was one, and it had a firm grip on me for years. That was one area where I meant my walk with God was a

AN OPEN BOOK

Struggle with Sexual Immortality

struggle. Let me explain to you my journey and how I was set free.

My journey with a sex demon began at the age of five. I know you are wondering how can a five-year-old have a sex spirit. To break it down, children are unaware of what spirits and demons are when they are young. They are innocent but demons do not care who they use or affect. There I was a young child just doing something unbelievable and wrong. Not realizing the reason or what was going on, a sexual urge came out of nowhere. I was exposed to pornography and masturbation. Where did it come from? I am sure now, but then I did not know. All I know

Struggle with Sexual Immortality

is it had me growing up feeling ashamed, confused, and scared. Often, I questioned how this happened to me and when did it begin. One day God showed me when it started and where it came from when I had spoken to someone about it.

Generational Curses

The spirits of masturbation and pornography came from a generational curse. For those who may not understand what a generational curse is, it is things that are passed down to children from family members. Let's say you may have come from a family who was alcoholics, and you began drinking and become one; that is a curse that

Struggle with Sexual Immortality

was passed down to you. It's many ways to describe it. I know some may not believe it but the world that we are living in is demonic and the devil is the prince of the air. That is why the word of God says, **For we wrestle not against flesh and blood, but against principalities, against powers, against the rulers of the darkness of this world, against spiritual wickedness in high places (Ephesians 6:12).** The evil forces of this world comes from Satan, and he tries to destroy our youth at a young age. He knows that if he can get our children young to get addicted to things, he can do whatever he wants to them. He cannot touch them because I pray daily over my children that God will

Struggle with Sexual Immortality

break every curse off my life so it will not be passed down to my children. I came from a family that had sexual lustful spirits. There was infidelity in marriages and pornography being watched. And I got exposed to it unknowingly.

This curse stuck with me until my adult years. When I became a born-again believer, I fought so hard, trying to break free, but I did not know how. For years I wrestled with those spirits, trying to walk in liberty. I would constantly think about it and it had me feeling miserable. One day, I was at work, and I began crying because I wanted to be delivered from that sex demon. This

AN OPEN BOOK

Struggle with Sexual Immortality

demon had a stronghold on me and would not let me go. It felt as if I was going to die in my sin. I knew what I was doing was wrong but still, I could not get free. As I was crying, I went into the bathroom to call my pastor. She then told me to calm down and gave me some instructions on what to do. I went to have a meeting with her that same week, and it was brought to my attention when I began having those sexual urges. She asked me when I started having sexual feelings. I explained to her at the age of five. She kept telling me it was a faith thing and a mind thing. I had to believe that I was free and proclaim it. I was ok for a while after that, but I kept falling short of indulging in sexual activities. Having

Struggle with Sexual Immortality

unrighteous intercourse, masturbation, and pornography had me feeling broken and worthless.

Dealing with that sexual spirit had feeling out of place. It was like I could not control myself. And when I would attend church, I would feel ashamed, as if someone saw what I was doing. As I sang in the choir and did other things for the church, I did not feel right. I begged God repeatedly to free me from those sins. Having nonmarital sex was hard for me because I tried pleasing God and the person I was with at the same time. I had a hard time telling men no when it came to sex. But I knew I needed to be free. I was

Struggle with Sexual Immortality

being a hypocrite with one foot in the church and the other out.

Some sins can have you so addicted to where they control you.

The more I tried to fight, the harder it was. As I said, I kept asking God to just end my life. He spoke to me and said, "no, no matter how many times you try to give up or fall short, my will for your life will be done." I have a great call on my life, and many things have been spoken over me. I am one of God's chosen to speak on and carry the Gospel of Jesus Christ. My mother is a pastor, and so was my father. My mom would always say it was prophesied that all her children would be

Struggle with Sexual Immortality

saved, and she stood on that promise.

I began to seek the Lord. The more I would seek Him, the more my desire for sex would die. I finally quit watching pornography, but it took a bit longer for the masturbating spirit to leave. One day, I was home relaxing in bed, and suddenly, a sexual urge came over me. I would often think of the scriptures **James 1:14-15: But every man is tempted, when he is drawn away of his own lust, and enticed. Then when lust hath conceived, it bringeth forth sin, and sin, when it is finished, bringeth forth death.** James 1:14-15 was one scripture that I always took to heart, and I still do. This scripture

AN OPEN BOOK

__Struggle with Sexual Immortality__

scared me because I did not want to die physically in sin or spiritually. You would think knowing those scriptures would stop you immediately from sinning. But again, that spirit was a stronghold. So, after I had sinned, I cried and prayed. I said to myself, no more, enough is enough. I believed that if I confessed my sin to someone else other than my pastor, I would be free. So, I called an older sister and talked to her and her husband about it. Her husband is a prophet and has always been like a big brother to me. I began to explain what I was battling with and how long I was battling with it. They began to pray with me and for me. I let everything all out, and afterward, I felt a heavyweight lift from

AN OPEN BOOK

Struggle with Sexual Immortality

from me. I believe that it was a stronghold for so long because every time I had fallen short, it would hit me hard. Several times as Christians, some people would stay down in their pity and shame. For me, every time I knew I sinned, it would take me a while to pick myself up again. I would not attend church if I sinned on a Saturday, or it would be difficult for me to pray or praise God. It was due to me not being able to accept God's forgiveness. Often, I would think to myself, what is the use because God will not hear my prayers, or I don't want to keep displeasing Him. I was so embarrassed all these years about this issue I had going on. But it felt so good to confess it and have someone to pray

Struggle with Sexual Immortality

me and not judge me. Usually, I would be ashamed even to let anyone know about my sins. I was not even going to write about my struggle with sexual immortality, but I felt led to because someone else is going through the same thing. Scripture says in **Romans 3:23: For all have sinned and come short of the glory of God.** There is no greater sin than the others. We are all faced with the same type of judgment on that day Christ returns. The decision for our life living would be either heaven or hell. Everyone has secrets they do not want to tell, but I am bold enough to share mines to help others be free. As I stated before, I understand that I am a light of the world, a city that cannot be hidden

Struggle with Sexual Immortality

(Matthew 5:14). As my life is part of the kingdom of God, I must tell my testimonies because someone else's deliverance and breakthrough, depends upon me. So, I encourage you that if you feel led to tell someone about what you have gone through, then do it. You may be the key to their deliverance.

Chapter 5
God Spared My Life

Unashamed

As I share many of my testimonies, one thing I must be grateful for is life. God has covered me and protected me so many times. If it were not for Him, I would have been dead and gone a long time ago. But I understand that long as you proclaim Christ and live for Him, the devil will always have a hit out for you. With many attempts, he tried to take me out in numerous car accidents. Death has knocked on my door several times, but God spared me, so I dare not to turn my back on Him. With everything

God Spared my Life

I have shared so far, as you can see, I am blessed to be alive. There were times God could have cut me off from the earth. Besides the things I mentioned, God's protection shielded me on the dangerous roads. I almost lost my life more than once on the highway. Therefore, I pray daily before I leave home.

During my first marriage, my husband, son, and I were facing a car accident. We had taken a family trip to Jacksonville, Florida, with some of my husband's relatives. On the way home, we decided to make a stop at the flea market. Florida is one state that has hot temperatures. Inside the flea market, it was so hot that I felt

God Spared my Life

like I was about to pass out. I got weak, and my husband had to carry me back to the car. If that was not bad enough, a wreck was waiting for us on the way home. We were riding down the interstate. The interstate has about four lanes. As we were traveling, we heard a loud noise, and our car started hydroplaning. We were spinning around in circles in the middle of the highway. Then the car came to a complete stop. A tire had blown, but the thing was, the oncoming cars were still coming. I was sitting in the passenger seat with my son sitting behind me. We were facing the traffic and all I could think was, "oh my God, we are about to get hit." As the cars flew by, they missed us. It

AN OPEN BOOK

God Spared my Life

had to be an angel that rescued us. When I looked out of the window, one car was so close to us, and I thought that was it for us. But instead, the vehicle quickly swerved around us. There is no way that car should have missed especially because of how fast it was riding. That is how I know the hand of God was upon us, but certainly not the last.

Another incident occurred on my way to church on a Sunday morning. I planned not to attend that day, but I felt it in my spirit I needed to be there. It had just finished raining. As I was driving, I am not sure what happened, but my tires slid, and my car hydroplaned so hard that mud flew through

God Spared my Life

my window. Then it hit someone's mailbox. The first thing I did was look in the backseat to make sure my kids were ok. And they were, but it did scare them. Also, my son's car seat was tilted over. I just started thanking God. I then went home to change, called my pastor, and told her what had happened, but we did thankfully make it to our church service.

Some years later, heading to a play rehearsal with my kids and a friend of mine kids, we got hit by a big pickup truck. I was trying to get across a busy intersection. There was a turning lane, and I was at a stop sign with the cars facing me in the turning lane.

God Spared my Life

This intersection is dangerous because it is hard to see any other oncoming vehicles. I looked both ways, and the person in the car in the turning lane signaled me that I could go before them. It looked clear, but soon as I attempted to cross the road, a truck ran into us hard. It was like the truck just appeared out of nowhere. It hit the passenger side of the car. The truck hit us hard but thank God no one was hurt. I was grateful that the driver of the truck did not press charges. As for my car, it was damaged and had to be towed. After weeks of waiting for my car to be fixed, it was not long after it was damaged again for good.

AN OPEN BOOK

God Spared my Life

A few months after that wreck in the same year, I got into another accident, but this time it was only me. Going to work early one morning, I got distracted by a small roach. This may sound funny, but I am a person who hates cockroaches with a passion. The roach crawled across my dashboard, and I tried to kill it. I was so distracted that I lost focus on driving. The next thing I knew, my car hit a brick wall. And it happened so fast that there was no way I could have avoided it. My vehicle got damaged and was not worth fixing because of the repair cost. What's so messed up is, I only had three more payments to make then it would have been paid off. I was so upset with myself for allowing

God Spared my Life

something so tiny to distract me. Even though it was my fault I hit the wall, a great woman of God reminded me that sometimes the devil would throw small distractions in our path to make us lose focus. It is so important that we always stay alert spiritually and naturally. Regardless of what happened, God blessed me by protecting me. He also allowed me to receive a significant amount of money from my insurance company. I was able to pay cash for another car that was even better than what I had before.

I have so many stories I can share, but I will mention one more about a car situation. My husband now and I were on the way home

AN OPEN BOOK

_____ **God Spared my Life** _____

from work on the interstate. I was driving and was driving about eighty miles per hour. Days before, I kept hearing a noise coming from a tire, we did not pay it any mind because it was a light noise. We worked forty-five minutes away from where we lived. So, getting off onto our exit, he pulled the car over, and my husband got out to look at the tires. He said one tire looked a little flat, but we could make it home. We made it home safely, and my husband said the Holy Spirit spoke to him and told him to look at the tires again. He checked all of them, and when he got to the driver-side front tire, he noticed the bolts were hanging off a little. He said they were so loose that when he touched them,

God Spared my Life

they fell right off. I said to myself, oh my God. We could have been in a terrible car accident. It was nothing but the grace of God that kept us safe.

We are not sure who could have loosened our bolts. It possibly was someone from the job because two other people's vehicles were damaged in the parking lot. One car had a sneaker bar in the gas tank, and the other one's tires were slashed. Someone on the job had to be messing with other folks' cars. And it was some crazy things going on at work. We asked if they had cameras, but they did not have any out in the parking lot. But I am just thankful for the mercy of God.

God Spared my Life

I know I shared several situations with almost being in a car wreck, but I must share the goodness of God. Being in situations where your life flashes before you is a scary thing. I got to let people know that He is honest and is a protector. I love God so much and owe Him all of me. He has been so good to my family and me. I am forever thankful for His grace and mercy and that I am still alive.

Chapter 6

Blessings and Sufferings

Unashamed

We all know that the year 2020 has been a year of sorrow and yet, blessings. I believe everything that has happened was meant to happen in that year. For one, God has shown Himself in many ways whether people were paying attention or not. God has given us time to get our lives right with Him and get ourselves together. Also, He has given us a chance to be blessed financially, but it has been our decision what we did with our finances. At least, that is what I believe.

I have gone through a series of heartaches, being judged, being told what I

Blessings and Sufferings

should do and what not to do. In 2020, I sacrificed and suffered a lot. Not just in 2020 but also over the years, I gave up things for the sake of the Lord and others. One area I suffered in drastically over the years was poverty. But in 2020, God blessed me more than He has ever blessed me before. Before I go into how my year was in 2020, I would like to give a little background of my poverty journey.

As I mentioned before, I came from a family that did not have much, and we lived in poverty for years. My parents struggled with nine children in the home. I always told myself that I do not want to grow up living

Blessings and Sufferings

in poverty. Poverty can also be a generational curse as well. And I believe it was passed down to me, and I thought I would never come out of it.

I graduated high school, as mentioned before, I moved to Norcross (Atlanta) Ga, and planned to go to college. Nothing happened the way I planned. I had a job, but it was minimum wage, and I could not afford to pay bills with that amount of money. I lived in Norcross for about three years, then had to move back home with my parents. I had lost my job because I did not have transportation to work.

Blessings and Sufferings

Over the years, I had different jobs, but none paid enough to pay bills or live independently. I was back and forth living with my parents. Even after I had gotten married and divorced, my living situation wavered for a long time. I relocated from place to place between friends and relatives. And there was a sense of guilt and shame on me for so long.

With being ashamed for years, I was a grown woman with two kids, not giving them a stable life. I felt like I was cursed. Growing up, my dad moved us from house to house and city to city for whatever reason. I thought maybe his habits fell upon me since

Blessings and Sufferings

I had a hard time keeping a home and finding a job that paid decently. When I finally found a job that paid well, my application would not get picked or required me to work on Sundays. I love God so much that I never wanted to miss church. I sacrificed turning down job opportunities because I had to work on Sundays.

I can say that God did take care of me when I did have my own home. Once, I did not have the money to pay my light bill, and I was on the verge of being cut off. One day I received a letter in the mail from my light company, and it said we have decided that it is unnecessary to disconnect your electricity

Blessings and Sufferings

at this time. I was so stunned at what I had read. I had to read it repeatedly. No one can tell me that was not the favor of God. When does a power company decide not to cut your power when it is overdue? The company I was with was faithful at cutting lights off on time.

In the circumstances of going through poverty, I had my days of being up and down. Although I went through, I could never give up on God. I had several jobs, but they would be about an hour away. And things would happen where I would have to miss work, and the year I got in a car accident twice was one of those years. The job would either be far or

Blessings and Sufferings

temporary. I then began to search for work closer to home, and I found one. I fell in love with it, and it paid well, but it was a temp. I later found myself back to square one, driving out of town. That year was the year 2019 and the year I met my husband.

Months after dating, we got an apartment together and worked for the same company. It paid three times more than any other job I've had. So, things were starting to get better in my life financially. I loved what I did. The work was easy but challenging. Things were going well until I heard the Lord speak to me and tell me to turn around, go home, and seek His face.

Blessings and Sufferings

The day I heard God tell me to go home, we were now in the year 2020. But let me back up a little. At the beginning of the year, my husband, and I were shacking by living together before marriage. We both felt convicted, so we decided to go ahead and do the right thing by getting married. Months earlier, we had already talked about marriage, but we had people telling us it was too soon. Even though people were telling us that, I knew it was the right thing to do.

I received confirmation that he was my husband, so I said, why wait? Both of us felt that way. I know individuals stick to the theory of maybe you should date for years

AN OPEN BOOK

Blessings and Sufferings

before marrying, but I do not believe that. When it is meant to be, long as you seek God and get the ok from Him, what others think does not matter. You can date someone for years and still not know the natural person. There is a spirit of deception that manipulates even Christians.

My husband and I decided to get married even if no one agreed with us. We decided to go to the courthouse. We planned to have a wedding, but we found out the place we chose to get married was unavailable. So, it was just the pastor and us. There were some congratulations, and there was some judgment.

Blessings and Sufferings

For months, we went through backlashes and persecution. Not just about us being married, but other personal matters. We suffered so much, but finances were not one of them. It was about three months we worked on our job. The morning I heard the voice of God speak to me, I thought it was just me. I had already missed two weeks of work. I had gotten an abnormal pap smear, in which the dr. told me it could be cervical cancer. That was devastating news to me, but I kept rebuking it and speaking healing over my body. I was not feeling well either and I found out I was pregnant.

Blessings and Sufferings

The morning my husband and I was going back to work, I had a conversation with God. When I heard Him say to me, turn around, go home, and seek my Face at first, I brushed it off. Then I heard Him say it again. I said but God, I have a bill that needs to be paid next week, He replied and said, don't worry about it. I said, but God I am making more money than I have ever made in my life, He said, I have more money than that, what you worried about? I responded again and said, ok God if this is you, you have to give me a sign. As I was getting off the exit to turn on the road towards our job, I began to feel pressure in my chest. I took it as a sign, so I told my husband what was happening, and he

Blessings and Sufferings

said Well, you better listen. Also, he said God had told him the same thing, He was just waiting on Him to reveal it to me. I knew God was pulling us off the job for ministry purposes. Yet, we still went back. The first day, we learned about the coronavirus, and the supervisor said that they would be laying people off. The next day, I discovered I was being talked about by the head people over the company I worked for. I was told I was on the verge of being fired. So, that took the icing off the cake. I said, ok, this is it, we are quitting for good.

While taking that leap of faith, quitting our job, I was worried about what

Blessings and Sufferings

others would think. God spoke to me and said, don't worry about what people say; they will think you all are foolish for quitting and wonder how you are making ends meet. And that turned out to be true. Some even thought that my husband was just sitting home not working but that was not the case. He was being obedient to God, and He blessed us all year long. There is not one time we were unable to pay a bill or feed our family. It is now 2021, and we are still blessed. See when you are faithful to God, He will be faithful to you. He must honor His word and take care of His own when we keep Him first.

AN OPEN BOOK

Blessings and Sufferings

The financial part of 2020 was one of the blessings besides healing taking place. I trust that God blessed us because we sacrificed and heeded to His voice, giving up our job. And with the benefits, there was some suffering. I mentioned that I found out I was pregnant. This pregnancy was my fourth pregnancy but my third child. I experienced a miscarriage with my first pregnancy. I went through so much in my body.

Before I found out about the pregnancy, I went to the ER for something and found out I had a fibroid. A fibroid is a harmless and cancer-less tumor. The nurse

Blessings and Sufferings

had told me it may or may not harm my pregnancies. When I found out I was pregnant, the fibroid had done grew along with the baby. It had grown to ten centimeters and was causing heavy bleeding during the first three months. The dr. explained that the fibroid would not harm the baby but was covering my cervix. They then referred me to a high-risk dr. I went to my first appointment, and they said the same thing. They went over what would happen if the fibroid did not move. If the fibroid did not move by the time I was in delivery, I would have had to get a c-section. But even then, where the fibroid was located, it could have caused me to bleed to death if they had to cut me in a particular

Blessings and Sufferings

area. I prayed and had others pray on my behalf. Two months later, I went back to the high-risk dr. She told me there is no need for me to return because the fibroid had moved out of the way. All I could do was give all the glory and praise to God. It was nobody but Him who allow it to be moved.

Close time to my delivery date, I did not dilate at all. My doctor scheduled me to be induced three days before my actual due date. I was a little stressed because I was huge and could barely do anything. I also had carpal tunnel severely. On delivery day, they induced me, gave me an epidural, and the pain was horrible, but I pushed through.

Blessings and Sufferings

Then, as my baby started dropping, the dr. said, "wait to push, there was an issue." The umbilical cord was wrapped around his neck, but thankfully God worked it out for me to have a safe and healthy delivery.

Just when I thought it was all over, I got some devastating news that my son had yellow jaundice. I had never heard of yellow jaundice, and so I read up on it. It is a common thing that some babies get after birth. The yellow jaundice was severe. His bilirubin kept rising and dropping back and forth. I barely had a chance to hold him. He had to stay up under blue lights, which was

Blessings and Sufferings

the therapy for the jaundice. It hurt to see my baby in that condition.

My husband left the day I was discharged. He left because he had ministry work to do, and I know it hurt him to see his son under those lights. Our infant looked so helpless. It was a long journey. I breastfed my son and then found out a week into still being in the hospital that it was possibly my breastmilk causing his bilirubin to go up.

I was angry at the dr. I felt like they should have told me that information the first day of finding out about the situation. I wanted to fuss but remained humble. We stayed in the hospital for over a week after I

Blessings and Sufferings

was discharged. I have nothing to complain about because with the prayers of the righteous, the nurses were still assisting me even after my discharge, and I was able to have alone time with God, I was alright. My son made it through, and that is enough to give God thanks. Even while suffering, I was still yet blessed.

For several months, entering 2021 things were still going great but I still had to endure some suffering. When you are anointed and chosen by God, you must endure some things. Things has been great, and we have not wanted for anything. Yet, there has been some attacks. Spiritually, God

AN OPEN BOOK

Blessings and Sufferings

has been calling me hirer in Him and suddenly, our finances were attack, our vehicle tore up, my husband went back to work but lost it months later because he had no transportation to work. I said ok, God, What is going on? He took me to scriptures about suffering for His name's sake and for ministry reasons. One scripture that helped me and encouraged me was **1 Peter 4:12-13 which says, Beloved, think it not strange concerning the fiery trial, which is to try you, as though some strange thing happened unto you, but rejoice, inasmuch as ye are partakers of Christ's sufferings; that, when His glory shall be revealed, ye be glad also with exceeding joy.** When we

AN OPEN BOOK

Blessings and Sufferings

go through things that are purposely to help push us into the next level in God, He said to think it's not strange. For His sake we are going to face difficulties and afflictions throughout life that will seem as if God is not there or seem like things will not get better. God tells us instead of giving up or complaining to rejoice because in due time things will get better. Our flesh must be broken and denied. So, in the mist of my sufferings and trials, I can't say there were not times I did not want to give up, but I had to press my way and keep going because of something God was trying to birth on the inside of me. It's just as a woman who is giving birth. As women, we suffer through

Blessings and Sufferings

changes in our bodies as our bodies prepare to give birth to our child. We have to suffer and endure the labor pain and contractions. And once we get pass that stage, our birth becomes completed, although some must heal from having a c-section. It's the same way in the spirit. God must cut away things from us in order for us to birth out things. Also, He cut away things to make us pure and righteous.

As I suffered, I had to go through the pain and push out my spiritual baby. In the end, the thing that God was trying to birth out of me was complete and He blessed me all over again. I constantly was reminded of Job

AN OPEN BOOK

Blessings and Sufferings

how he suffered many afflictions, but he never gave up on God. It was necessary for him to go through what he did. Sometimes it's necessary for us to go through to help us and to help others. We are witnesses of Christ and because He suffered, we are required to suffer as well. But no matter what trial we face, God will never suffer us to go through anything we cannot handle. Besides, it was for my good. Through my sufferings, I have become stronger in God, and I can feel His presence stronger on me. It's great to have money and it is needed, but to be rich in the spirit is greater than being rich with coins. I'd rather have the riches of God any day and allow my soul to prosper.

Blessings and Sufferings

I have grown and have learned to be patient and learned how to endure and go without. In the book of **Philippians,** Paul speaks of going without and having plenty. Even though I went through a time of being without, God still provided. And since I remained faithful, God restored. My husband was blessed with another job that pays well and our finances increased. Also, I have been blessed with having my own business, so God never failed me. He was just preparing me for greater. So, I encourage you that if you are going through a season of being without or suffering, press through it without complaining, because God has something waiting for you at the end of your trial.

Chapter 7
More Than a Conqueror

Unashamed

Nay, in all these things we are more than conquerors through Him that loved us (Romans 8:37). This scripture has been a help to me through many of my battles. Everything I have faced, believing that I am an overcomer, has brought me out of those dark places. And it is only by the blood of Jesus I am a survivor. Our life is a faith walk because the test and trials we must endure can get us through living for Christ.

God has told us in the word that we will suffer many afflictions. And there are times we can also put ourselves in situations

More than a Conqueror

that are not ordained for our lives. If I had made wiser choices, some things I went through would have been avoided. That is only if it was not from God. I went through a dark path of unforgiveness and being ashamed of my sufferings. It took God to help me cope with my mistakes and move forward.

Now that I am more mature in God, I have learned from my downfalls, accepted my tests and trials, and realize that my life is a living testimony. I know there are so many others who have gone through some of the same things I have. **Scripture says in 1 Peter 5:9, Whom, resist steadfast in the faith,**

More than a Conqueror

knowing that the same afflictions are accomplished in your brethren that are in the world. And for that reason, I want my light to shine in helping people overcome their issues. It is my ministry to let others know that they can be set free and delivered.

God let us know that there's nothing too hard for Him. When we live for Him, walk in obedience, and love Him. He will fight every battle. We do not have to face anything alone. The devil is already defeated. God has given us power and authority over the devil. The only way the devil can defeat us is if we allow him to. Sometimes we can give our strength and energy to him. Many

AN OPEN BOOK

More than a Conqueror

times, we are tried and tested, and we know it be a test, still we give in to the temptation.

For example, I remember working on this job and the supervisor would constantly nag me and find something to pick at me about. It was as though she tried everything to get on my nerves or maybe the enemy was using her to try and make me act out of character. One day I had enough of her nagging. She came to me that morning and complained about something and she said something that pushed my buttons. It took everything in me not to retaliate. I was so upset. But, instead of responding with words, I left. I decided to walk off the job before I

More than a Conqueror

lost my cool and get out of character. It was best for me to just quit that job. I did not tell her; I left without saying a word or clocking out. You see I am a person where it takes a lot to get me to a certain point before, I explode. That day, I was about to, so I had to leave. I knew that if I would have given in to the enemy's plan, I would have said some things I would have regretted. I thank God for humbleness although it took me a while to get there.

There is no demon or devil that God cannot overpower. It does not matter whether it is sexual immortality, unforgiveness, hatred, bitterness, or etcetera, all these sins

More than a Conqueror

can be conquered. I have battled with many sins, but I allowed God to help me to be free from them. Therefore, I will let it be known where I came from and how I broke free. I pray to God that I can help many overcome their situations through my testimonies. And to those who may be carrying a heavy weight of any type of sin, say this: **I AM AN OVERCOMER!** Keep repeating it until it becomes personal and make you free. It will be a heavy burden lifted. Let this be the beginning of walking in liberty of the Lord.

A Prayer for Freedom

Dear Heavenly Father, I thank you for the opportunity you have graced me with to be a living testimony to others. Father, thank you for being so merciful and good to us. I pray for anyone battling with any rejection, sexual immortality, suicidal thoughts, depression, low self-esteem, poverty, or any other sins that may have them bound. Lord, please help them to overcome anything that is a stronghold to them. You said in Your word that Your grace is sufficient to us. I speak life and freedom over their circumstances. Where You are, there is liberty. Thank you, Lord, for the love and for the freedom I have in You, in Jesus' Name I pray, Amen!

Psalm 119:46:

I will speak of thy testimonies also before kings, and will not be ashamed.

SCRIPTURES RECAP

1. <u>Hebrews 11:1</u>: Faith is the substance of things hoped for, the evidence of things not seen.

2. <u>Revelation 12:11</u>: And they overcame him by the blood of the Lamb, and by the word of their testimony and they loved not their lives unto death.

3. <u>1 Corinthians 13:4-7</u>: Love is patient, love is kind. It does not envy, it does not boast, it is not proud. It does not dishonor others, it is not self-seeking, it is not easily angered, it keeps no record of wrongs. Love does not delight in evil but rejoices with the truth. It

always protects, always trusts, always hopes, always perseveres.

4. <u>1 Corinthians 7:8-9</u>: I say therefore to the unmarried and widows, it is good for them to abide even as I. But if they cannot contain, let them marry; for it is better to marry than to burn.

5. <u>Psalm 8:2</u>: Out of the mouth of babes and sucklings (infants) hast thou ordained strength because of thine enemies, that though mightiest still the enemy and the avenger.

6. <u>Galatians 5:7</u>: For the flesh lusteth against the Spirit, and the Spirit against the flesh, and these are

contrary the one to the other, so that ye cannot do the things that ye would.

7. <u>2 Corinthians 12:9</u>: And He said unto me, My grace is sufficient for thee, for my strength is made perfect in weakness. Most gladly therefore will I rather glory in my infirmities, that the power of Christ may rest upon me.

8. <u>1 John 4:4</u>: Ye are of God, little children, and have overcome them; because greater is He that is in you than he that is in the world.

9. <u>James 1:14-15</u>: But every man is tempted, when he is drawn away of his own lust, and enticed. Then

when lust hath conceived, it bringeth forth sin, and sin, when it is finished, bringeth forth death.

10. Romans 3:23: For all have sinned and come short of the glory of God.

11. Romans 8:37: Nay, in all these things we are more than conquerors through Him that loved us.

12. 1 Peter 5:9: Whom, resist steadfast in the faith, knowing that the same afflictions are accomplished in your brethren that are in the world. And for that reason, I want my light to shine in helping people overcome their issues.

13. **Deuteronomy 31:6**: **Be strong and courageous. Do not be afraid or terrified because of them, for the Lord your God goes with you; He will never leave you nor forsake you.**

14. **1 Peter 5:9**: **Whom, resist steadfast in the faith, knowing that the same afflictions are accomplished in your brethren that are in the world.**

Other Books

Unforgiveness, Guilt, and Regrets "Scars of the Past" (available on www.booksaddition.com, Amazon, Lulu.com, Barnes&Noble.com, Walmart.com, Book Dispository.com, Target.com. and more

Women of Confidence "Poetic & Devotional Book" (available on www.booksaddition.com, Lulu.com, and more to come)

Next project: Entrepreneur Magazine

www.ingramcontent.com/pod-product-compliance
Lightning Source LLC
Chambersburg PA
CBHW071212160426
43196CB00011B/2275